URANUS

MURRAY "OAK" TAPETA

NORWOOD HOUSE PRESS

Cataloging-in-Publication Data

Names: Tapeta, Murray.
Title: Uranus / Murray Tapeta.
Description: Buffalo, NY : Norwood House Press, 2026. | Series: Outer space | Includes glossary and index.
Identifiers: ISBN 9781978574953 (pbk.) | ISBN 9781978574960 (library bound) | ISBN 9781978574977 (ebook)
Subjects: Uranus (Planet)--Juvenile literature.
Classification: LCC QB681.T374 2026 | DDC 523.47--dc23

Published in 2026 by
Norwood House Press
2544 Clinton Street
Buffalo, NY 14224

Copyright © 2026 Norwood House Press
Designer: Rhea Magaro
Editor: Kim Thompson

Photo credits: Cover, p. 1, 5, 7, 18 NASA Images; pp. 6, 12, 13 Vadim Sadovski/Shutterstock.com; p. 8 See U in History/Shutterstock.com; p. 9 imageBROKER.com/Shutterstock.com; pp. 11, 17 buradak/Shutterstock.comi; p. 14 VGstockstudio/Shutterstock.com; p. 15 Golubovy/Shutterstock.com; p. 21 MNStudio/Shutterstock.com;

All rights reserved. No part of this book may be reproduced in any form without permission in writing from the publisher, except by a reviewer.

Printed in the United States of America

Some of the images in this book illustrate individuals who are models. The depictions do not imply actual situations or events.

CPSIA compliance information: Batch #CSNHP26: For further information contact Norwood House Press at 1-800-237-9932.

TABLE OF CONTENTS

Where Is Uranus?..4

How Was Uranus Discovered?...8

What Is It Like on Uranus?..10

Has Uranus Been Explored?...19

Glossary...22

Thinking Questions...23

Index..24

About the Author..24

Where Is Uranus?

Our **solar system** has eight planets. Uranus is the seventh planet from the Sun. It is the third biggest planet. Uranus is 63 times larger than Earth!

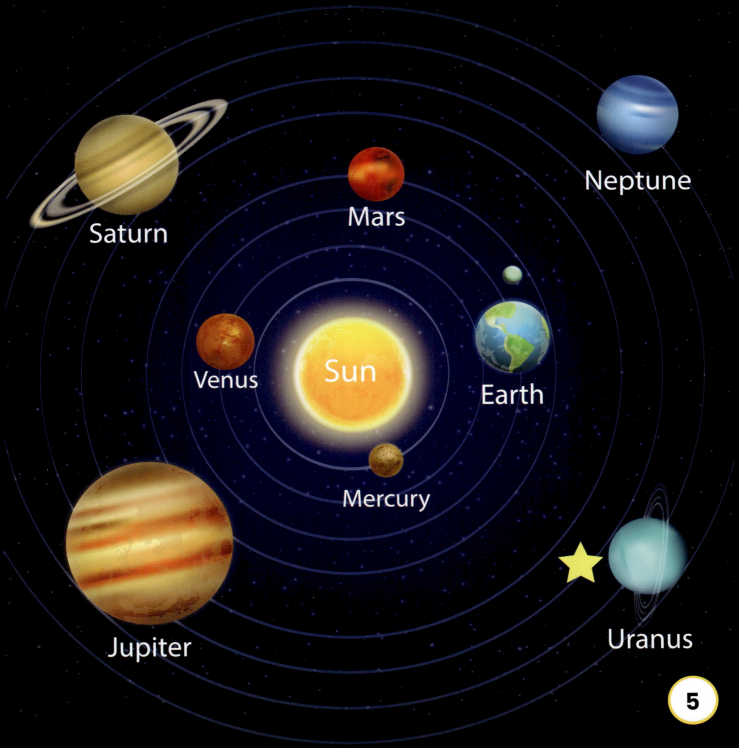

Uranus is nearly two billion miles (nearly three billion kilometers) from the Sun. Getting from Earth to Uranus would take at least four years.

One year on Uranus is about the same as 84 years on Earth. It takes Uranus that long to **orbit** the Sun.

How Was Uranus Discovered?

Ancient people could see Uranus only when the sky was very clear. It looked like a small, blue-green star. They named the planet Uranus after the Greek god of the sky.

German **astronomer** William Herschel first saw Uranus through a **telescope** in 1781.

What Is It Like on Uranus?

You could not stand on Uranus. It does not have a solid surface. It is made of flowing, icy materials. At the center is a small, rocky **core**. Uranus is sometimes called "the ice giant."

Uranus has 28 moons. There may be more moons to discover. The planet also has at least 13 rings.

Uranus is very windy. It is the coldest planet in our solar system. The thick **atmosphere** is made of the gases **hydrogen**, **helium**, and **methane**. Methane makes the planet look blue.

Gravity on Uranus is a little weaker than on Earth. If you weighed 100 pounds (45 kilograms) on Earth, you would weigh 86 pounds (39 kilograms) on Uranus.

Scientists think Uranus formed nearly five billion years ago. Gravity pulled together swirling dust and gas. Over time, a planet formed.

Long ago, something big may have crashed into Uranus. It might have caused Uranus to tip over. Uranus is the only planet in our solar system to spin on its side.

Has Uranus Been Explored?

In 1986, the **satellite** *Voyager 2* flew by Uranus. It sent photos back to Earth. It collected data. It is the only spacecraft that has been close to the planet.

Astronomers want to explore Uranus more. For now, they use powerful telescopes to study the ice giant. There is water on Uranus. Scientists want to know how it got there.

Glossary

astronomer (uh-STRAH-nuh-mer): a scientist who studies objects in the sky, including planets, galaxies, and stars

atmosphere (AT-muhs-feer): the mixture of gases that surrounds a planet; air

core (kor): most inner part; center

gravity (GRAV-i-tee): an invisible force that pulls objects toward each other and keeps them from floating away

helium (HEE-lee-uhm): a light, colorless gas that does not burn

hydrogen (HYE-druh-juhn): a gas with no smell or color that is lighter than air and that easily catches fire

methane (METH-ane): a colorless, odorless gas that burns easily

orbit (OR-bit): to follow a curved path around a larger body in space

satellite (SAT-uh-lite): a spacecraft sent into orbit around a planet, moon, or other object in space

solar system (SOH-lur SIS-tuhm): the Sun and everything that orbits around it

telescope (TEL-uh-skope): an instrument that helps people see distant objects

Thinking Questions

1. Where did the planet Uranus get its name?

2. Describe the weather on Uranus.

3. Why is Uranus called "the ice giant"?

4. What may have caused Uranus to tilt over?

5. What satellite helped explore Uranus?

Index

atmosphere 13

Earth 4, 6, 7, 14, 19

gravity 14, 15

Herschel, William 9

moons 11

orbit 7

rings 11

Sun 4, 6, 7

telescope 9, 20

Voyager 2 19

About the Author

Murray "Oak" Tapeta was born in a cabin without plumbing in Montana. Growing up in the great outdoors, he became a lover of nature. He earned the nickname "Oak" after climbing to the top of an oak tree at the age of three. Oak loves to read and write. He has written many books about events in history and other subjects that fascinate him. He prefers spending time in the wilderness with his dog Birchy.